D1178808

Chats
with
Cats

Chats
with
Cats

How to Read Your Cat's Mind

Celia Haddon

Little Books by Big Names™

First published in the United Kingdom in 2004 by Little Books Ltd,
48 Catherine Place, London SW1E 6HL

10 9 8 7 6 5 4 3 2 1

Text copyright © 2004 by Celia Haddon
Illustrations copyright © 2004 by Gray Jolliffe
Design and layout copyright © 2004 by Little Books Ltd

A CIP catalogue record for this book is available from the British Library.

ISBN: 1 904435 31 9

The author and publisher will be grateful for any information that will assist
them in keeping future editions up-to-date. Although all reasonable care has been
taken in the preparation of this book, neither the publisher, editors nor the author
can accept any liability for any consequences arising from the use thereof, or the
information contained therein.

Many thanks to: Jamie Ambrose for editorial production and management,
Claudia Dowell for proofreading,
Mousemat Design Limited for text design,
Printed by Scotprint in Scotland.

Cartoons hand coloured, using
the TRIA system by LETRASET

www.letraset.com

I may well read this – if I have time…

'That's it: create a distraction while
I go and steal a sausage.'

CONTENTS

AUTHOR'S NOTE

I am always coming across new information that increases my basic understanding of feline behaviour – from experts, from books, from readers and, of course, from my own cats. Thus, when my publisher suggested an expanded edition of one of my earlier books, it seemed a good opportunity to pass some of that new knowledge on to my readers.

This book is therefore a revised and updated version of *How to Read Your Cat's Mind*, which was written more than three years ago. Although it is, at its heart, the same book, it contains many important additions – including more fascinating feline facts and, crucially, some better explanations of just what it is that makes cats behave as they do.

INTRODUCTION

Love is… hearing your cat purring. Like the half-shut eyes and the rough, painful touch of a cat's tongue, purring means all is right with our world: the world of the cat-human bond. As the mysterious vibration reaches our ears, we would purr back – if we could.

What a gulf separates us – the clever upright apes who have learned to travel in space – from the small, desert carnivores who cannot even use words. Yet love spans this great divide, linking two different species in a loving relationship. We spend our lives together, most of the time with contentment. Indeed, the cat-human relationship sometimes works better than marriage.

Does your cat properly understand you? It probably does – well enough, at least for its own purposes. It can lead you to the fridge, persuade you

to change the brand of cat food, wake you up in the morning to make sure its breakfast isn't late, and share your bed on cold nights. It may even know how to move you off the most comfortable chair.

Do you understand your cat? Probably not as well as it understands you. This book will help you chat to your cat – in a language it understands.

It will explain the cat's basic instincts, the way it talks and what it means; how, what and when it learns. It will outline what a cat needs to have a happy home, and explore some of the common misunderstandings in the cat-human relationship to help you make your cat happy. It will also describe some of the special needs of pedigree cats and of cats kept indoors. And finally, it will help you pamper your elderly cat.

The happiness of your cat really matters.

Is that something to eat down there?

chapter one
BASIC INSTINCTS
IN THE CAT YOU LOVE

You may think your cat is a sweet little darling. You may wish to treat it like a cuddly pet. But cats have instincts: wild and mysterious. They are not soft toys. If you forget this, your chats with cats won't get you very far and may lead to real misunderstanding on both sides.

The cat that sleeps on your bed and lies upside down under your central-heating radiators is a relative newcomer to human family life. Unlike the dogs, horses, cattle and sheep that have been domesticated animals for thousands of years, cats moved in only recently.

Domestication occurred about 6,000 years ago – at the very most, 10,000 years. This is not very long in evolutionary terms. And we probably didn't domesticate them; they domesticated themselves, walking into our lives when there were enough mice and rats in human settlements to make it worthwhile for them.

Indeed, you could argue that cats domesticated us. They get shelter and cat food, and in return they haven't had to change many of their habits. *We* are the ones who have changed. It has taken a few thousand years for them to persuade us, but now they don't even have to pay for board and lodging by doing the rodent control.

Clever cats: we give and they take. How did they pull off this amazing trick?

PET SHOP

'I'll have that one.'

Your cat's heritage

If you want to understand the sheer cunning of the pet cat, you have to know a little about its heritage. Your cat, even if it has a posh pedigree, is still a wild cat at heart.

It was descended from the African wild cat about 4,000 to 10,000 years ago. The original cat ancestor still flourishes in the desert. It is more or less the size of a domestic cat, with a coat varying from grey to tan. We don't know much about it because it is not a spectacular animal like a lion, and it's difficult to track.

We know that the female cats live in with their kittens, until these are old enough to leave the family group. But while lions hunt in family parties, so as to pull down game as big or bigger than themselves, the African wild cat hunts alone, killing mainly rodents, some birds and other small animals. There's no reason for group hunting; a single mouse isn't big enough to feed more than one.

The wild cat is a cat that hunts by itself. And this affects cat behaviour. A wolf needs its pack in order to kill for food, so it learns many social tricks needed for group living. Home is where the pack is. Not so the African wild cat.

The males roam widely, more or less on their own, while the females live with their kittens. But,

'So sue me.'

'You can't touch me – I'm a protected species!'

as far as we know, adult African wild cats have never lived together in large communities.

The wild cat needs a territory, not a pack. Home is an area within a wild cat's territory where it is safe, where it has its kittening dens and its places to sleep during the day. This is the core territory.

Further afield are its hunting grounds – its home range – where it can hunt without too much competition from others. If prey is scarce, this territory will be a big one, up to four kilometres. If there are lots of rodents, it will be a small territory.

At the edge of its territory will be the boundaries where other cats may be found: either competing females or males roaming in search of sex. There is little to see on these boundaries, but the African wild cat, like all cats, will leave scent marks of various kinds. As territory will always be more important for survival, rather than social bonds, the wild cat needs to mark its own territory and to recognize the territories of other cats.

How the wild cat came in from the cold

The African wild cat is different from other smaller wild cats; it can be tamed. Other cats, like the very similar European wild cat, stay aloof when grown, even if they are reared by humans. An African wild cat reared by humans seems to accept them as family.

Nonetheless, from the start when the first African wild cats began to live near or in human settlements, their relationship to humans was very different from that of the other domesticated animals. Cattle were herded or penned up, and then eaten by men. Dogs were used by early man as guard dogs and as hunting assistants – although the game they pulled down was primarily to feed men and they only got the bits left over. The pack instinct had betrayed them into obeying human instructions.

Cats never did this. The bolder ones moved into human settlements of their own accord, and were welcomed for their ability to get rid of the mice and rats that overran grain stores. But humans didn't exploit the cat's hunting activities; mice were of no use to the human larder.

So cats were left to hunt on their own (just as they did in the wild). They were not trained, controlled, tied up or otherwise put in cages or fields. They lived side by side with humans, each species conferring a benefit on the other. It was a remarkably equal relationship.

It still is.

'You scratch my back, I'll scratch yours.'

Cats still live on the wild side

Of course, today's household cats are no longer African wild cats; they have changed both physically and mentally. Their coats come in beautiful colours and they are no longer entirely solitary by nature – feral and stray cats prove that. If there is enough food, such as a nearby rubbish dump or a friendly feeder, strays will live together, not in a pack, but in family groups within large colonies.

Perhaps this family-group living, which allows cats to live happily in human families, is a change brought about by domestication. Or perhaps the African wild cat had this potential but its lifestyle – catching small rodents in desert areas – usually made group living impossible. Another possibility is that domestication encourages kitten-like behaviour, making it natural for cats to live with their mother in a little family. Just as dogs behave more like juvenile wolves than grown-up ones, so pet cats behave like juvenile wild cats rather than adult ones.

Eating habits may also have changed the domestic cat. The true African wild cat rarely

'Suddenly I'm in a "multi-cat" household –
and I only have myself to blame.'

scavenges or feeds on rubbish dumps. But domestic cats are found on rubbish dumps throughout the African wild cat's territory. They have developed a digestive system more able to cope with dump food.

Today's domestic cat has the ability to live in social arrangements which would not suit a wild cat. Many can live happily in a multi-cat household, sharing beds and grooming each other, although some individuals will still be happier living as a single pet.

The tiger in your cat

Your own petted and pampered feline shares the same instincts as its wild cousin the tiger – instincts which are hard-wired into its brain. There are three of these:

- The sex and kittens instinct
- The hunting instinct
- The safety instinct

Unless you understand that these three instincts shape your cat's lifestyle, you will never be able to chat to your furry loved one. These instincts are common to all cats everywhere: pampered pets, posh pedigrees, street strays and lonely ferals.

A cat is always a wild cat at heart.

Sex and kittens – we can fix this

This instinct – mating and reproduction – is now under human control by means of neutering and spaying. This drastic measure is the only way of stopping the instinct at source. Cats that are not neutered are escape artists when in search of sex – as the small ads for 'pedigree-cross kittens' reveal.

Most domestic pets are not allowed to breed, but the ready supply of kittens at cat rescue shelters (often the offspring of stray or feral cats) suggests that nothing we humans do is seriously going to reduce the worldwide stray-cat population. We may snip, but on the streets stray kittens still flourish.

Neutering and spaying are essential for those who want a relaxed and close relationship with a pet. And, in a world where thousands of cats end up in rescue shelters, it is selfish to insist on yet another litter of kittens just for human amusement.

Besides, un-neutered tomcats are noisy, smelly and roam around looking for copulation, often getting into fights as a result. Female cats are so extraordinarily fertile that a single female can produce 200 kittens in her lifetime. If all those kittens survived, there would be as many as 65,536 extra cats in the world five years later. Neutering allows our cats to enjoy the deep peace of the warm house instead of the hurly-burly and excitement of life and love on the rooftops.

True sexual behaviour does not survive neutering, but some of the reproduction behaviour – mother or kitten love, for instance – remains. Cats will use the language of family love in the cat-human relationship, treating us either as kittens or mother cats.

'I've been neutered.'   'Me, too – but let's go for it anyway.'

The hunting instinct – we can't change it

Your cat (and every cat) has the mind of a murderer. It is designed as a killing machine. Cats have to eat meat; their digestive system can't get enough nourishment out of a vegetarian diet, so nature has programmed the cat to live to kill.

We feed our cats lavishly so that they have no survival need to hunt for food. But nature hasn't caught up with tinned cat food, and our dearest Puss is still a killer at heart. There's no need to starve cats to make them better hunters. The best-fed cat in the world, faced with a mouse, will hunt it down.

Furthermore, a hunting cat is a happy cat. Fulfilling its instincts fires up the happiness section of its brain. Your cat doesn't have to catch any prey to enjoy it. Even if it is an indoor cat that has never seen a mouse, it will enjoy play-hunting.

The hunting programme, installed by nature into the cat's brain, is a set sequence of moves. These occur in a predictable serial order, one action succeeding another, as given on the next page.

•See or hear prey.

•Eye prey.

•Stalk prey. This can take some time, with the animal slinking, then stopping to look. There is sometimes a final fast run forward.

•Pounce on prey and grab. This is often a grabbing bite, or the victim may be held down by a paw with claws out.

•Bite prey. This is the killing bite at the nape of the neck.

•Tear off skin or feathers.

•Eat.

All these actions are immensely rewarding and fulfilling for the cat that performs them. Happiness for a cat is doing what it was designed to do: hunt.

The hunting sequence is almost a compulsion. Each action follows the other; sometimes one move can't be performed until the previous moves have preceded it. The sequence often stays in its set order.

Watch your cat make a pounce that fails to locate the mouse; it rarely pounces immediately again. It is much more likely to go back to move one (eyeing its prey), then do a shortened version of move two (the stalk) before it pounces for the second time.

We call cats cruel for the way they torture wounded mice on our lawns. But the cat isn't cruel. It is compulsively performing its predatory sequence, which its brain is designed to perform. Unless a cat is distracted by something, when it sees moving prey it *has* to stalk and pounce.

The need for the hunting sequence to stay in order also occurs when a well-fed domestic cat grabs the prey but fails to kill-bite it, either because it isn't hungry or because the mouse isn't in the right position for the nape of the neck bite. At move three (the pounce and grab), the sequence comes to a halt. Then the cat begins once more at move one (eyeing the prey), starting the whole sequence again – over and over. This is the dazing of the mouse, which often upsets us humans.

'There's a limit to the things you can
do with a mouse before you kill it.'

Yet the dazing has a purpose. Positioning the mouse correctly for the nape bite is important, for if the cat bites the back end of its prey rather than the nape of its neck, the mouse may turn round and bite. Even a small mouse bite can turn into an abscess which, in turn, may affect the hunter's ability to hunt. So nature has hard-wired the cat to wait till its prey is in exactly the right position for the kill.

Sometimes a cat simply can't proceed through its complete hunting programme because the stimulus for triggering the next move isn't there. It is the prey's movement that usually starts off the cat to stalk and pounce. Cats only learn by experience – not instinct – how to pounce on motionless prey, and a pet cat that doesn't do a lot of hunting may not learn how to do this.

So if a small mouse that is being 'played with' by a cat freezes motionless, the cat stops pouncing. Its hunting sequence has been interrupted by the prey's failure to move and trigger the next action. Besides, since even a small mouse bite may diminish hunting efficiency, the cat's behaviour has been designed to keep the mouse in play until it is definitely too tired to bite back – although hungry cats have an incentive to cut short the play-with-prey routine.

The same behaviour is seen when our cats eye, stalk and pounce on a cat toy. Most cats ignore a static toy; we must move it for them. Or they will move it with their paw before they can stalk and pounce on it.

For cats that have no opportunity to hunt, playing with cat toys is an important release. Cats which don't have enough pouncing, grabbing and tearing in their lives may start developing weird behaviours (more of that later).

In the meantime, there is nothing we humans can do to change the cat's tendency to hunt. We can take the cat out of the hunting field, but we can't take the hunter out of the cat. This is because nothing is more rewarding for a cat than hunting. It is innately pleasurable – even if the performance is truncated and there is no fat, juicy mouse at the end.

The safety instinct

A cat's way of avoiding danger is to have a safe territory. To feel secure, a dog needs a pack, whether human or dog. Yet for an adult cat, security doesn't come in the shape of a companion, whether feline or human; it comes in the shape of a territory and, in particular, the core territory to which it can retreat in complete safety.

Core territory has hiding places where a cat can sleep undisturbed; it has scratch marks where it can leave a message for itself or others; and it has different kinds of scents put there by the cat itself. Home must *smell* like home for a cat to feel safe. Outside your cat's core territory is a wider, looser territory that is its hunting and patrolling range. This may overlap with other cats' territories.

Within the home territory and hunting range are latrine areas where the cat can relieve itself without fear of ambush. These are usually in the safe sector of the territory, because a cat that is

'Just so there's no confusion,
this is *my* territory.'

squatting cannot run away. The smell of these areas is reassurance in itself, and sometimes cats are happy to share latrine areas.

But, just to confuse us humans, defecation and urination are also used to mark territory features and boundaries. Marks are usually left by spraying urine upright, rather than squatting, and sometimes by defecating and leaving the dropping in full view. Other territory marks are left by rubbing or by scratching; more on these later.

Any time danger threatens, all animals (and humans, too) have four options. To remember these, it's easiest to think of them as four words all beginning with the letter 'F': fight, flight, freeze and fiddle about (i.e. do something – any appeasement behaviour – which might make a killer decide not to kill you).

Fighting is costly because in the wild (where there are no vets) an injured animal can easily die from blood poisoning from even a small wound.

Animals that survive by hunting will starve if they get too injured to hunt successfully.

Moreover, cats are small creatures. They haven't a hope in a fight with anything bigger than themselves. Even with something near their own size, like a Jack Russell or a fox, they are likely to come off with very severe injuries if they survive. Nor, with their small size, can they succeed in bluffing it out by a threatening show of force – although they will try this if necessary.

So for your cat, turning to fight is a last resort. Backed up in a confined space, it will hiss, claw and bite, but its preferred strategy is flight. Most cats aim for flight up something, like a tree, because they are not good long-distance runners. High places make them feel safe, if they cannot hide out of sight.

Even before the flight reaction, their way of coping with anything worrying is to keep a safe distance. They will sit close to a friendly cat, but far away from a stranger cat, and will come nowhere near an animal which might be an enemy. You can tell how your cat feels about another cat or another person by the amount of distance it keeps between itself and them.

Indeed, your cat will try to avoid danger in the first place. Most cats are neophobic: very cautious in new places, fearful of new people and new things. The shock of a new territory – for instance when the humans move house – sends many cats to hide under the bed.

Ignore your cat's basic instincts and you will have a stressed, unhappy cat. Work with its instinct, and your cat will be happy and relaxed.

'Don't you like your nice new cat food?'

'If that's it, can I go?'

chapter two
HOW TO CHAT TO YOUR CAT

Your cat understands you. It has probably worked out how to ask you for food and also how to get you to open a door for it. Some cats even let their owners know when it is time (in the cat's opinion) for bed. A surprising number have mastered the tricky business of waking up their owners for a regular 5AM snack.

All this and they don't even use words!

You, for your part, probably know when your feline friend is feeling miserable. You can recognize an ill cat. You know when your cat is particularly enjoying its meal. You know when you have irritated it.

Yet our two species are using foreign languages to chat with each other. We humans primarily use a complicated series of vocal sounds: words. Tone and pitch of voice vary the meaning. We also use body language as a form of expression. Communication by scent, common among animals, is minimal among us; we can learn very little by giving another human being a good sniff. We have a very poor sense of smell.

Cats, on the other hand, chat primarily by body language. Secondarily, they use vocal noises. Tertiarily, they use scent and tactile contact. Scent messages between cats say a lot and are well understood. Scent messages from a cat to human are often ignored or misunderstood. As well as keener hearing and a better sense of smell, cats have a tactile sense organ: whiskers. These are used more to receive information than to send it.

The better you understand cat-chat, the more you will understand your cat.

'I'm only trying to communicate…'

How to read cat-chat signs

When humans use body language to convey messages, the main area of communication is the face: smiles, frowns and tears. Dogs also use facial language; they can wrinkle their brows, smile, hang their tongues out, and their facial expression transmits mood messages recognizable to humans. Cat faces are relatively immobile and are difficult for humans to read correctly. Yet there are some signs to read.

'Cagney, say hello to your new friend!'

Ears and mouth chat

Ears can convey both fear and aggression – *if* we can understand them. A relaxed but alert cat has its ears forward and erect. The ears go sideways and downwards as a gesture of appeasement in a frightened cat. A cat which is aggressive keeps its ears erect but swivels them backward. As the aggression (and fear) increases, the mouth opens to show the teeth that might bite. A terrified cat, ready to fight, has ears that are so far back they are barely visible and teeth very much on display.

Eye chat

It is not polite in cat society to stare. A cat that wishes to avoid aggression will avoid eye contact, often by turning its face to one side. Blinking or narrowed eyes is another way cats show politeness.

Eyeball to eyeball confrontation shows potential aggression between two cats. A cat which retreats with a fixed stare is telling the enemy that, if cornered, it will fight. For this reason, humans who wear spectacles should take them off if dealing with a frightened cat. Blinking and looking away will also be reassuring.

The cat's fear of glaring eyes may also partly account for the way they go towards people who dislike cats. Those who dislike cats tend not to make eye contact with them.

Intense watching, but not eye-to-eye staring, is also part of the predatory sequence and may precede a play pounce on another cat.

Body postures chat

Cats don't live in a pack so they don't have the variety of body language a dog has. Dogs have a whole range of movements they can make which tell another dog that they know their place, whether high or low, in the pack. Cats don't have this pack language. They put distance between each other, rather than doing appeasement body language.

However, cats do express their emotions with their bodies. Most of us humans can recognize the message of alarm and aggression in a cat that has its back arched high, its fur fluffed up, and its tail low. Obviously this is a cat that is trying to make itself look big and threatening by fluffing up its fur. In order to get the message of maximum size across, the cat will often stand sideways on.

The frightened cat that is hoping not to fight back does just the opposite. It lowers its whole body to the ground, to make itself as small as possible. This is a signal to show an aggressor that it doesn't want a fight. Its ears are down and flat.

Human beings normally loom over cats. One way to reassure a frightened cat is to lower one's body into a crouch or even lie flat on one's tummy. This is body language that says 'I mean you no harm'.

Then there is the interesting feline body posture known as the social roll. A cat will lie down, exposing its tummy to another cat. This can be used as an invitation to play or as a defensive gesture with all claws ready to strike. Some cats also use it to say 'Please don't hurt me; I am only little'. A hostile cat looming over the rolling cat will usually withdraw.

The social roll can be used as an attention-seeking move towards humans, who can rarely resist responding to it. Some cats (and they are probably in the minority) then enjoy a tummy tickle. But a human who unwisely tries to tickle a cat's tummy may find his or her hands caught in the feline rake where the cat's hind legs kick and claw at the hand. The tummy is a particularly sensitive spot for most cats.

Tail chat

The normal tail position of a cat going about its business is horizontal or slightly lowered. But there is a tail-up greeting message, where a friendly cat comes towards its companion (human or friendly cat) with its tail held high often with slight curve forward at the very tip. This tail-up greeting is not found in wild cats and it may have developed (like the canine smile) during domestication.

Tail-up is also used during body rubbing (which also has a scent message) as the cat weaves itself round human ankles. Normally a cat rubbing round its human's legs is trying to get human attention.

A forward tail tip curve is friendly. But there is also a hostile hello in which the bottom half of the tail is raised outwards, but the main part of the tail is curved downwards. Before a fight, the hostile cat will pull its tail downwards to get it out of the way. The crouching, terrified cat has its tail tucked right out of sight. No cat wants to risk damage to its tail, which is so essential for signalling and for balance.

A cat that is twitching or lashing its tail is usually considering attack. Tail twitching or lashing normally occurs before the pounce, during the cat's hunting stalk. It also occurs if a cat is contemplating an attack on another cat or a human. If you see your cat lashing its tail, stop whatever you are doing.

Finally, the tail plays a part in sexual signalling. A female cat on heat will crouch, with its backside raised towards the male. Its tail is held to one side. Pet cats sometimes do a flirty version of this to their humans. They present their backsides but with the tail up, in the friendly-greeting posture, rather than held aside in the sexual come-on signal.

Claw and paw chat

Cats keep their sharp claws sheathed and walk on their toes. Claws come out to help them run up trees or to attack. They are used as a weapon during the predatory pounce. Dogs give a paw as a friendly gesture, but a cat with its paw slightly lifted, is ready to cuff you! A human with a hand outstretched may look threatening to the cat.

'All yours, Freddy – I had the last one.'

Vocal chat

In human vocal language, each word has a series of meanings; if you're not sure what a word means, you can look it up in a dictionary. There is no dictionary for cat language. Cats have a vocal vocabulary, but it is much less important than body language, and it may not be common to all cats. Your cat has acute hearing; it can hear a mouse's footfall. But it usually only recognizes a limited number of human words and may rely as much on tone of voice as word recognition. Cats vary in their use of sounds to chat, but there are some recognizable calls.

Chirrup. This is a little chirrup or trill used as greeting between cats and their kittens, sometimes to humans.

Purr. Used when nursing kittens or as a response to being touched. It can be switched on by physical nearness of humans, by good food or by soft surfaces. Some cats purr almost silently. Some cats purr to their humans even when in pain or frightened.

Meow. An attention-seeking noise that varies in length. Meaning varies with context and individual cats. Orientals use long meows frequently. Some cats meow silently.

Growl. A warning sign of aggression.

Yowl. On a rising note, a warning, angry or complaining sound.

Hiss. Defensive tone often meaning 'back off'.

Spit. A more violently defensive sound.

Chatter. This is an involuntary excited predatory noise, made when a cat is watching prey.

Caterwauling and sexual calls. Neutered and spayed cats don't need these.

There are cats that rarely make any sound at all and cats that will use only one or two sounds to their humans. Siamese and oriental breeds may meow almost all the time they are with their humans.

Older cats are usually more vocal than younger ones. They have learned that humans respond better to sound than to body language or scent marks, so they use the meow more frequently and more loudly than in their earlier years.

Yet there isn't a fixed meaning to a meow. Individual cats may use a slightly different-sounding meow for different occasions or contexts, i.e. one meow for food and another one for a request to open the door. The meaning varies with individual cats. There is also a kitten distress meow: a call to the mother cat used when a kitten is in difficulties.

Touch and scent chat

In addition to calls and body language, cats use touch and scent. Many scent messages need tactile contact to be delivered. Most tactile messages also spread scent, and the scent component may be as important as the tactile contact.

Though cats have a sense of smell that is less keen than that of dogs, they nevertheless have a better one than humans do. When a cat delivers a

tactile scent message, most humans receive the tactile message but miss the scent that goes with it. They simply cannot smell well enough to notice it.

There are scent glands all over the cat's body: beneath the chin, on the cheek, at the corners of the mouth, at each side of the forehead, at the base of the tail and between the cat's toes. These give off a scent which most humans cannot perceive but which are easily perceived by another cat. When a

cat rubs against another cat or its human, it leaves some of its scent behind. It also picks up the scent of its companion on its own body, mixing the two scents together.

This mixed scent is the smell of family or home to a cat. It is very important. We recognize our friends by their faces, but scent is the way a cat identifies friends and foes. A family member who smells wrong may be wrongly identified as an enemy. For instance, a cat which has been to the vet and smells of the hated veterinary surgery may be attacked as a hostile intruder by a cat left at home. It may look the same, but it smells 'wrong'.

Grooming also probably plays a part both as a tactile and a scent message. The scent from saliva would be left on the groomed cat's fur. Clearly, grooming between cats is a sign of friendship; enemies don't groom. So if your cat insists on licking you, take it as a compliment, even if it is an uncomfortable one!

The following are the main scent messages.

Rubbing. This spreads a scent from the cat's skin glands. Cats rub with their chins, cheeks, foreheads, flanks and tails. They rub other cats and humans, mixing this scent with their own. They rub marking points in their territory.

Spraying. Entire tomcats spray, but so do neutered males and females at times. The cat stands at full height, arches its back, and squirts a jet of urine at a vertical surface.

Middening. The cat uses faeces to send a message and to mark territory. The faeces are left uncovered as a visual as well as scent signal.

Scratching. The scent glands between a cat's toes leave a smell on the scratched area. Scratching is also a visual signal.

The only scent messages that get through to the human nose are the 'pee and poo' ones. Cats can probably read the gender and sexual status of the cat that left them. They may also be able to read the time

'That's right, Sam – you tell 'em!'

the message was left. So urine and faeces to them are a kind of bulletin board, providing useful information.

Humans, however, get very upset and sometimes insulted by these messages. Yet cats don't leave them to offend or insult. Inside the house, they are usually a cry for help from a cat that is very worried indeed. Spraying and middening indoors are the ways cats try to reassure themselves by marking their territory. But they are a problem for humans (more of that later).

The other problem for humans (not cats) is scratching. Scratching trees, furniture or carpets leaves both a visual signal and also a smell, since there are scent glands between a cat's toes. A scratch is also a message board for another cat passing by. Humans can see, rather than smell, this message, although they don't understand what it says.

Cats also scratch in the presence of others, and it may be an ostentatious display of confidence. When one cat has finished scratching, its companion may then take its place at the tree. Cats that scratch furniture in front of their owners have discovered a way of getting human attention, if not approval.

How to chat to your cat

The key to understanding any foreign language is practice – and this is true as well for both humans and cats. An inexperienced cat will be better at reading our body language than our vocal words. But an experienced cat can understand some of our words: the 'vet' word, for instance. (Why else do they disappear when hearing it?) And the more experienced a cat is around humans, the more words it knows and the more it uses its voice to get through to us.

If you want to communicate better with your cat, you can use some of its own signals. With a frightened cat, you can be careful to give it only sideways glances – not a glare. You can also try to become lower than the cat; let it get up higher on to a table or shelf, while you go down to ground level, flat on your tummy.

Inexperienced humans often spend a good deal of effort trying to understand a cat's vocal chat when they would do better to concentrate on its body language. You have probably learned some of its body language already, even if you don't know you have done so. Careful attention to its ears and gestures will give further information.

Finally, you can even leave a scent message for your cat. By petting it, you are giving it your scent and taking on some of its own. Nowadays, it is even possible to buy an artificial pheromone that will help you leave reassuring scent messages for your cat on furniture or household cat pathways.

'If you don't want me on your chair,
what's with all the pheromones?'

chapter three
BRINGING UP BABY

From the moment you bring home a new kitten, you are teaching it how to behave, whether you know that or not. And, although you won't realize it, your kitten is teaching you how to behave, too. Most cats manage to train their humans rather better than their humans train them.

The idea that cats can't learn is ridiculous. Every single experiment has shown that cats are remarkably quick learners – *if* they want to be. If they don't want to (and often they don't), then they won't bother to learn. The lesson must be suited to their nature.

For instance, it is easy to teach a gun dog to retrieve a dead bird, because the dog has had the retrieving instinct bred into its breed for hundreds, if not thousands, of years. It is also happy to be out in the fields with men with guns. It would be extremely difficult to teach a cat to retrieve game, because it has not been bred to do so. It would be frightened in unfamiliar territory, terrified by the noises of guns, and scared by the presence of strange human beings. Cats, unlike dogs, are not much reassured by the presence of their owners.

'The first thing you learn as a cat is to
pretend to never learn anything.'

Love lessons for your kitten

Long before it even arrives at its new home, your kitten has learned several lessons. Indeed, the behaviour of any adult cat is defined by its experiences in kittenhood.

The single most important lesson that your pet cat needs to know is how to love human beings. If it doesn't learn this as a kitten, it may never learn it for the rest of its life. It will always be wary around human beings and will grow up as a feral cat.

Most feral cats have had dysfunctional kitten-hoods, brought up without human contact. They can't be handled. They will avoid humans, except for cautious approaches if food is left down regularly.

There is a window of opportunity in kittenhood when a cat can learn that humans are friends. Tiny kittens do not know fear. You can handle them and cuddle them much more easily than older cats. For the first few weeks they are little care-eliciting babies. Their demeanour, their little cries, their chubby shape, are nature's way of getting their mothers, or their humans, to look after them.

This fear-free window is called the 'sensitive period' and it falls between the second and seventh week of kitten life. The process of accepting a different species as a friend is often called 'socialization'. Socialization has to happen before kittens get the fear instinct. This instinct kicks in around the eighth week, growing stronger until the fifteenth week.

Thus, during the five-week period before it knows fear, your kitten needs to be handled by at least four different humans, preferably including men, women and also children. The more handling your kitten has had, the friendlier it will be in later life to humans. It also needs to get used to the smell of humans, since smell is important for the feline identification of friend or foe.

If it is to be adopted into a home with a dog, your kitten also needs to meet a friendly dog during this period. And if it is going to be happy in a home with lots of other cats, it needs to meet other adult cats, not just its mother, during its kittenhood. It needs to learn how to handle social life. An only kitten, brought up in isolation with just its mother, may become a bit of a loner and will be happier as a single pet.

Finally, during this sensitive period your kitten also needs to get used to human noises, household smells and ordinary human activities. It will learn that it need not be frightened by the noises of the washing machine, the telephone, the radio and the TV. The ideal home for a kitten is a noisy household with children, friends who visit, a calm, loving dog, and one or two other cats. Growing up in this atmosphere will mean that your kitten is used to, and not frightened by, most domestic activities.

The worst upbringing for a pet cat is to be born in the wild. Stray kittens that are rescued off the street need a lot of handling as early as possible by their rescuers to overcome their fear of humans. Rescuers who don't realize this may hand out kittens for adoption that will grow up to be wild animals. Wild animals can sometimes be tamed by endless human patience, but they rarely make easy pets.

The other bad upbringing is that of a pedigree kitten that is reared in a cat chalet, a shed or a quiet spare room. Kitten farms, where kittens are produced cheaply en masse for sale to pet shops or via small ads, produce physically sick and emotionally stunted kittens. But even some pedigree breeders who love and cherish their cats simply don't understand the importance of exposing their kittens at an early age to human life in all its forms. Unscrupulous breeders will show the buyer their kittens in the house, but then stick them back into the shed when the would-be buyer has left.

So although your kitten has a posh pedigree, the pedigree alone will do it little good. Only a good education, with lots of handling, will make for a happy pet.

Food, litter and other early lessons

Your kitten learns a lot from its mother in the first few weeks of its life. At four weeks, it starts eating solid food and learns from its mother what it should eat. Researchers discovered that if a mother cat had been trained to eat bananas, her kittens learned to enjoy bananas, too – therefore a kitten that has been brought up on only one type of food will prefer that type in later life. A kitten that has been offered a variety of different foods will be less fussy about what it will eat as an adult.

Hunting is also picked up by observation. A mother cat starts bringing her kittens dead prey when they are about four weeks old. Later she brings in live prey and helps them hunt it down. So a kitten that is fed on birds by its mother will prefer to hunt birds.

However, the hunting instinct is so strong that kittens which have never come across living prey can nevertheless learn to hunt even late in life. A pampered pedigree cat that has been brought up on tinned food all its life will be a poor hunter to start with, but in time it will learn to catch mice. The basic instinct is that powerful. You cannot normally train a cat to stop hunting living prey.

Litter preferences also start early. Kittens begin to use litter around the age of five weeks. If they are placed on litter, they will begin to dig it, and they get used to the smell and the feel under their feet of whatever is in the litter tray. If your kitten was introduced to wood chips, it will probably prefer wood-chip litter as a cat. A kitten given sand will prefer sand.

Finally, there is the weaning experience. As the kittens eat more solid food, they begin to grow teeth and their mother is (naturally) less keen on being suckled. When they are about seven weeks old, she will begin to refuse them her nipples. Thus, by being refused milk, the kittens learn to eat solid food.

They also learn another very important lesson. As they are refused their mother's nipple, they experience times of frustration when they can't get what they want. The mother leaves them or lies down hiding her tummy. She starts refusing their overtures. They are left to cope without her help.

This experience of frustration is important. It will enable them to tolerate other frustrating experiences later in life without losing their emotional cool.

Bottle-fed kittens sometimes miss out on this frustration experience. Even if the bottle is withdrawn, humans offer soft food immediately in its place. These kittens never experience a refusal; you could say that they are like spoiled children who are never thwarted. As a result, they may grow into cats that cannot tolerate frustration. These cats use their claws on humans to get their own way.

Although the most important lessons take place before the age of eight weeks, cats can learn some of them after that time; it will just take longer for the lessons to be learned and they may be learned less thoroughly. It is therefore important to influence your new kitten's behaviour as early as possible.

However, you cannot work wonders. Cats, like humans, are influenced not just by their education but also by their genes. Some cats are naturally more aloof than others. You can make an aloof cat confident around humans, but you cannot make it enjoy cuddles.

I'm not aloof. I'm a cat.

Training your kitten with love

The secret of training your kitten is to start early. If you have two homes – a town flat, say, and a weekend country cottage – you may want a cat that is not frightened by car travel. In this case, the best plan would be to get a kitten as near the age of eight weeks as possible and accustom it to being driven by car from the beginning. A rescue shelter, if you explain this, may well be helpful.

But many pedigree breeders will not let a kitten go to its new home until it is fourteen weeks old. You might therefore ask the breeder if she will drive it around in the first few weeks of its life. If she refuses, you will just have to accustom it to car travel as soon as possible. And, to make sure that it becomes accustomed, it would be worth driving it around a little every day, not just at the weekend, for the first two or three weeks.

The experience should be made as pleasant as possible. Small items of particularly delicious food should be offered when the kitten is first put in its travelling box. The box can also be sprayed with

Feliway®, an artificial scent that is used to promote relaxation in cats.

The same procedure is necessary for a cat that is being taught to wear a leash. In this case, the harness should first be put on before meals; only when the cat is completely used to being in the harness should it be taken out with it – first into safe places and only slowly into more challenging places. It must also be remembered that harnesses (unlike collars for dogs) are not entirely safe. A truly terrified cat can almost always wriggle out of one.

Nail clipping, teeth cleaning, and intensive grooming for long-haired cats should be started as early as possible and performed frequently. The younger your kitten, the quicker it will become accustomed to these. Each experience should be made pleasant with good food treats.

You can also teach your kitten good manners. One mistake that is often made is to encourage a kitten to play rough games with humans. It is so sweet to see it pouncing with its claws out or even inflicting a tiny bite. The wound is so small that it hardly seems to matter at all.

But when your cat is an adult and it continues the same rough games, the pain can be quite intense. If you mistakenly punish the cat, you may find that punishment simply increases its aggression. For this reason, it is important from the earliest days that games using claws or teeth are not allowed. The game stops immediately at the first sign of these.

Ambush games should also be discouraged. It is amusing to see a tiny bundle of fluff hurl itself against a large human being. When a full-grown cat dashes from the bushes and rakes your legs with its claws, however, it is no fun at all. Ambushing games are particularly delightful for cats since they are based on the predatory sequence, a basic instinct that ensures that performance is always rewarding.

'I know you're there!'

The kindness principles

As a way of disciplining cats, punishment is out. Dogs may stick around for punishment, but cats won't. Pain or fear will totally poison your relationship with your cat, because it is unlikely to understand why pain is being inflicted.

Remember that cats avoid danger whenever possible, so rather than risk punishment from you, your cat may just decide you're not a safe person to be near. It may feel that its home is not a safe place to live in and respond by scent marking with urine or faeces. Or your cat may just pack up and leave home in order to find a new home without what it considers to be abusive human behaviour. Only dogs, betrayed by their pack instinct, stay around for more punishment.

Your cat (like all animals) will respond much better to rewards than punishment. But to do this, you have to learn what is rewarding to your individual cat. What you think is rewarding is not necessarily what the cat thinks is rewarding. Petting, or tactile contact, is very important to us, but usually less rewarding to a cat. Nor are cats, like dogs, anxious for our approval. Verbal praise will not be motivating.

The three most motivating rewards for a cat are:

•*Food*. The better the food, the greater the reward. Prawns motivate behaviour much more than bits of a cat's normal diet.

•*Attention*. Most pet cats enjoy human attention. If you want to encourage behaviour, respond with attention.

•*Games*. The predatory sequence of eye, stalk and pounce is innately rewarding to all cats.

There is also an alternative to punishment known as 'non-reward'. Non-reward, as the behaviour experts call it, is a powerful tool for changing animal behaviour. It is not punishment; no pain is inflicted – only disappointment. If a cat is expecting a titbit or attention and does not get it, it will learn to avoid the behaviour that did not get the expected reward.

These are three ways of using discouragement as a non-reward.

•Refuse to give the food reward which your cat knows you have ready.

•Ignore your cat – deny all eye contact, stay silent, turn the whole body away or walk out of the room.

•Stop playing the game.

Take, for an example, the constant yowl of a Siamese cat. Normally, humans respond to the cries in several ways: they pick the cat up, they talk back to the cat, or they may even shout a rebuke. All these responses are human attention, and for an attention-seeking cat, even a rebuke is a reward.

But the cries will be reduced if you never, ever give attention when the cat is yowling. If your cat is noisy, you should not pick it up, or shout at it, or even look at it. Walk right out of the room or turn your eyes and body away from the noisy animal in 'active ignoring'.

'Silence unnerves them…'

To encourage silence, pay attention to your cat only when it is silent. By doing this, you are using a reward of attention for silence and using a non-reward of ignoring the cat for unwanted yowling.

In the same way, if a rough game is halted, a cat will learn to stop the clawing that has ended the game. Continuing the game would be a reward; ending the game is a non-reward. Thus, games with sheathed claws can be encouraged by the continuance of the game: a reward. Games with unsheathed claws are terminated: a non-reward.

Yet even with knowing all this, changing cat behaviour is difficult. The main difficulty lies in the fact that we humans find it difficult to think like cats. We don't time our rewards or non-rewards correctly. We think a cat understands us far better than it does.

For instance, people often say 'Bad cat!' in a threatening tone of voice to a cat that is scratching the furniture. From the human point of view, this is a punishment, but a confident cat may well think of the rebuke as a reward – it has successfully got its owner's attention. It stops scratching temporarily because now it has achieved its aim: human attention. But it will scratch again when it wants its human to notice it again. Scratching achieves its aim.

Training a cat to do 'tricks' is far more difficult than training a dog. It has to be done with rewards because a cat will just walk away if it is punished. It requires human skill and patience, but it can be done and can be very enjoyable, particularly for an indoor cat. Your indoor cat will enjoy jumping over an activity course, following a laser light, offering a paw, sitting up on its hind legs, or lying down.

To sum up: there are five golden principles of training a cat.

•Never use physical or verbal punishment. Your cat will avoid you. Use non-rewards instead.

•Use rewards that the individual cat desires. Not all cats are motivated by the same things.

•Never force, however gently, your cat to do something. Train without touching your cat.

Instead set up a situation so that your cat does what you want, then reward it.

•Get your timing right. Your cat must be rewarded *exactly* at the time it performs the desired behaviour. This is tricky. Rewards that come too late are ineffective. Your cat cannot link them with its behaviour.

•Clicker training usually solves most timing difficulties. Get a book on this technique.

Good trainers, usually using clicker techniques, have taught their cats (at home – not for public performance) to strum the piano, to open doors or even to meow to music. And their cats have been purring all the time.

Best of all, by using clicker training to teach tricks, your cat can let you know when it has had enough, by simply walking away.

'It's clever the way you taught her to do that.'

chapter four
PEDIGREES AS PAMPERED PETS

Pedigrees benefit humans, not cats. From your cat's point of view, being pure-bred or having champions in its bloodlines has no value at all.

Cat shows are run by humans for humans – not for cats. Cats aren't snobs or celebrity-seekers. They don't care if they win or lose, and every single cat in a cat show would prefer to be hunting a mouse rather than sitting in a dull cage being admired by passers-by. Your pedigree cat will always be happiest when it is treated as a proper cat – not as a beautiful object on show.

Most cats were just mousers until 1871, when the artist Harrison Weir held the first big cat show at Crystal Palace, London. He hoped that cat shows would improve the status of cats, which at that time were treated far less well than dogs.

If shows really did achieve a higher status for cats, then this is perhaps the only real benefit they have given the feline race. The business of showing has also cost individual cats dear. Many have lost their freedom to roam and their freedom to hunt. They still have their freedom to reproduce, unlike many neutered pet cats, but this involves heavy restrictions for stud cats, often imprisoned in cat chalets rather than in a household because of their habit of spraying.

Worse still, once an animal is a pedigree, it belongs to a restricted gene pool. Persian can only mate with Persian, or Burmese with Burmese – though many, given the chance, would go out on the tiles and have exciting sex with a stray or even a feral. Some breeds came into existence with only a few foundation animals, with the result that this particular gene pool was incredibly limited even at the very beginning of the breed. A small gene pool means that animals have genes in common with those with whom they mate. The so-called 'hybrid vigour' – the natural good health and resistance to anatomical defects that comes from breeding like with unlike – is not for them.

Cat breeders usually refuse to breed from animals that are clearly weak, diseased or impaired. But an apparently healthy cat can carry recessive genes for a disorder. If that cat mates with a cat free from the gene, the disorder never shows up. But if it mates with a cat that is also a carrier (a situation that is more likely in an inbred gene pool), the disorder will become evident, transmitting noticeable inherited weaknesses or diseases to the kittens. Thus, inherited disorders become more and more prevalent, as the artificially restricted gene pool never takes in new blood.

It gets worse. The business of showing cats restricts the gene pool even further. Successful breeders often 'line breed'. This means that they will mate son to mother or cousin to cousin in order to fix a particular look that has gained prizes in the show ring. The resulting kittens are therefore further inbred.

Even without deliberate line-breeding, success in the show world has a tendency to reduce the gene pool. A stud cat that wins in a major show will be chosen to mate with more females than a less successful stud, so his genes will predominate in the kittens sired for the next few years.

This wouldn't matter so much if cat shows chose the healthiest and most robust animals as champions

– but they don't. They choose the prettiest. Energy, fitness and ability to mouse are not awarded prizes. Winners don't have to function well; they just have to look good.

Judges can make things worse by choosing the cat that is 'most' Persian or the 'most' Siamese. They look for what is called 'type'. Persian cats in 1871 looked much like ordinary cats, with ordinary noses but with longer hair. Now they have snub noses like pug dogs, and there is even a strain called ultra-Persians whose noses are so smashed back against their face that many have breathing difficulties, faulty teeth and running eyes. The worst-affected cats may have to be fed liquidized food.

Similarly, Siamese used to look more or less like ordinary cats, except for being a little lighter in build and having different colouring. Now they have been bred to be ultra-thin cats with long, tapering, wedge-shaped heads.

Brothers and sisters under the skin

Pedigree cats behave like ordinary cats – *if* they get the chance. Their hunting instinct is still there. Persians have a reputation for being poor hunters, but this probably arises from the fact that so many are kept as indoor cats with no chance of practising their skills.

Max, a Persian cat that lived in a canal boat with his family with free access to the bank, was a good example of a hunting Persian. He once brought home seven mice in one evening, having eaten one or two on the bank beforehand. He regularly caught young rabbits, shrews, voles, mice, frogs, toads and even rats – just like any non-pedigree cat.

Yet most Persians cats seem to be relatively lethargic. One reason may be that they have been bred for placidity in the show ring. The other reason why they may differ from ordinary moggies in their behaviour is simply because they cannot breathe so well. Cats with the extreme flat face may not be able to draw in enough oxygen to their lungs, so they cannot help but be lethargic.

'Ayatollah is a pure-bred Persian prizewinner, but
he hibernates between events.'

In contrast, there is one real behaviour difference between Siamese and ordinary felines. The Siamese, and the breeds developed from the Siamese, have a tendency to be more vocal than ordinary cats. Those who love the breed say that they are 'talkative'. Those who find the constant meowing difficult, consider them to be over-demanding. Siamese, or those breeds with Siamese blood, may also be far more prone to strange disorders such as wool-sucking or eating odd substances. More of that later.

More worrying than these behaviours, however, are one or two disorders that are showing up in breeds. These include:

•Polycystic kidney disease, or PKD. This disease is high-risk in Persians and exotics; medium-risk in several other breeds. Some kittens die at birth, and those that do survive die relatively early with kidney disease. Ultrasound tests are now available for breeders, so do not buy from untested stock or breeders who deny knowledge of the disorder.

•Gangliosidosis, or GM1 and GM2. This is an enzyme deficiency in American (not UK) Korat cats and American Siamese. A test is now available, so do not buy from untested stock.

•Heart disease. Possibly inherited in American Maine Coon and American Shorthair cats and more frequent (though maybe not inherited) in flat-faced cats.

Of course, not all inherited diseases occur in pedigree cats only. There is also a disorder that occurs frequently in white-coated cats, whether they are pedigree or not. The gene, or one of the genes for white colouring, is linked with a gene for deafness. It is commonest in cats that have white coats with blue eyes. Completely deaf cats should be kept indoors for their own safety, but otherwise, they can lead normal lives.

Some other breed differences are less clear. Burmese, for instance, may be particularly sensitive and anxious. But this apparent breed difference perhaps arises simply because cat breeders do not understand how to rear pet kittens. Some breeders fail to appreciate the importance of proper kitten socialization before the age of eight weeks. Their kittens may be bred in a cat chalet or in a quiet room, and handled by the breeder only, rather than by several other people.

Pedigree cat-lovers like the idea of giving extra-special care to their animals – not realizing that a rough-and-tumble regime is far better for the future pet. The kittens produced under the pampered, isolationist regime will always be relatively fearful and nervous adult cats. Thus, what appears to be a breed behaviour difference is simply the result of a bad upbringing.

We then blame nature for what is actually our bad nurturing.

'...so the snail
looks at the tortoise
and says...'

'The in-breeding
makes him funny
with strangers.'

Hair – hot or not?

Hair makes an obvious difference to behaviour, as cats try to cope with the extremes of too much or not enough of it. Both extremes can cause difficulties or discomfort to the cats involved.

Sphynx cats, a hairless breed, always seek out warm surfaces and are happy in, rather than on, the bed with their owner. They need seriously warm living quarters; should they be allowed out of doors, they also require the feline equivalent of dog coats. Rex cats, which lack the outer layer of hair, will also need more warmth. Sometimes cats of these breeds are born without whiskers and are thus deprived of an important sense organ.

Conversely, all long-haired cats, whether pedigree or not, will be far less likely to be lap cats. Wearing a thick coat, especially in a centrally heated house, they seek out cool places rather than the warmth of body contact with their owners. Long-haired and semi-long-haired cats are more likely to be found stretched out in an attempt to lose heat, rather than curled up in an attempt to preserve warmth. In hot weather they may need air conditioning, or at least a fan.

They also require regular grooming. A Persian will need grooming daily, while even a semi-long-haired cat needs grooming every other day. If you do not groom your cat, hairballs will often form in its stomach, and your cat may become constipated and lose its appetite. It may also vomit up the hairballs – probably just where your foot first lands in the morning when you get out of bed!

A long-haired cat that is not groomed has fur that begins to mat very quickly. The mats tighten, pulling at the roots of the fur, and soon the skin under the mat becomes sore. Once the mats have been allowed to form, grooming becomes painful for the cat and, naturally, as soon as it sees the grooming tools, it will run away. It will be afraid of being handled, and grooming becomes more difficult. A vicious circle has been set up.

To persuade your cat to accept grooming will take weeks of retraining, using a programme of rewards and endless patience. But it can be done. Deal with any existing mats with the help of the vet. Then lay in some very, very tasty treats. Allow a week or two or even longer for each stage. Patience is the key. Do not hurry this process.

Accustom the cat to being touched by a non-grooming item, such as a banana, while you hold a treat in front of the cat. Touch-then-treat for several days. Over several days, start moving the banana through the hair. Pretend to groom and treat with it until the cat is completely relaxed about the procedure.

Next, move to a soft brush. Holding the treat in the left hand, let the cat nibble it while you gently brush the cat's back with it. Only when the cat fully accepts this brushing should you proceed to brushing the neck ruff.

Then, retrain your cat to accept brushing below. Hold the treat at ground level so the cat almost has to lie down to reach it. Say 'Lie down' while you do this. When the cat lies down, give the treat. When this response is established, hold the treat and brush a little along the side of the body before giving the treat.

Hold the treat so that the cat has to lie on its back to nibble it. Then brush round the tail a little, while it is still nibbling. Most cats will respond by moving their back paws nearer the head, thus exposing their tail area.

Once the ordinary brush is accepted, you can change to using a slicker metal brush or even a comb. If mess is getting caught on the backside fur, consider clipping this with blunt scissors. This will need two people, one to hold the cat, one to cut. Be very, very careful.

'I was neutered years ago!'

The indoor cat

The other behaviour difference between pedigree and non-pedigree cats has nothing to do with their shape or breed. It is just that pedigree cat-owners are more likely to keep their cat indoors all the time, denying it access to the great outdoors. Indeed, some breeders will only sell kittens if these are to be kept indoors all their lives.

An indoor cat is protected from disease and will lead a longer and healthier life than a cat that is allowed out of doors. This physical health, however, comes at the cost to the cat's psychological health. If your cat is a solitary indoor cat, without daytime human companionship, it will probably be bored. It is deprived of all opportunities to exercise its hunting instinct, and is therefore more likely to develop behaviour problems than outdoor cats.

You can do a lot, however, to help your cat lead a better life indoors. Try to incorporate the following into your indoor cat's life.

Scratching post
Provide these. Spray with catnip spray if your cat needs encouragement and if it is sensitive to catnip. Consider buying a post with a carpet-lined hidey-hole higher up. This will give your cat a chance to practise its climbing skills.

Play
A cat needs to work off its predatory instincts in play. Get a fishing-rod toy. Throw balls of paper or kitchen foil. In the wild, a cat would hunt about ten mice a day, so aim to give your cat thirty pounces every day.

Toys
These don't have to be new or complicated. Christmas-tree balls are easy to bat, so are ropes hung from the ceiling; cats love cardboard boxes with holes to get into, and many like newspapers to claw. Put dry food into puzzle feeders. Good shop

toys include crinkle bags, fur-covered mice, etc. Easy toys to move are best. Change toys daily.

Watching
Make sure your cat can look out of the window and see other things. Put a bird feeder up for it to watch; you can buy some feeders that stick to the glass. Provide sitting places – on ledges and shelves at the window – with a view of passers-by, dogs, wildlife, other cats.

Food
Give food four times a day, if possible. If cats were in the wild, they would have to stalk and hunt for food. Get rid of the food bowl. Hide dry food around the house so that your cat has to hunt for it.

You could also build a food pole, like those used to feed the big cats in zoos which attempt to give environmental enrichment to their animals. Tigers and lions climb up these poles to get the raw meat at the top. A cat food pole consists of a trunk-like pole with holes bored in it towards the top. These can be filled with treats or dried cat food. Start with shallow holes, so that the food is easily pulled out, then make them deeper once the cat has learned what to do, so that it has to work harder for its meal.

Train your cat

Clicker training or ordinary tricks will fire the reward chemistry in your cat's brain. Don't train for an audience – just do it for good fun for both of you. Make an agility course. A clicker-training book will explain how.

Some people train their cats to chase a laser light, thus performing the eye, stalk and pounce of the hunting sequence. Unlike chasing a toy, however, the cat can never 'catch' or even touch its imaginary prey, which means it remains essentially unsatisfied. Some experts worry that too much light chasing may subsequently make some cats over-excitable.

'I don't think the cat thinks you're
trying to think like a cat.'

chapter five
HOME IS WHERE THE FELINE HEART IS

Cat rules are different from human rules, so from the start of the relationship, your cat is acting under a wholly different set of ideas. It is living by cat rules. What seems like common sense to you looks like idiocy to your cat. And what seems like perversity to you is good behaviour to your cats. So if you are to chat to your cat, you must definitely learn its rules.

Humans, with all the arrogance of a supposedly superior species (tell that to your cat!), expect domestic animals to fit into their lifestyle. They bring cats into their homes and expect them to follow a human timetable and human rules. The human decides whether the cat shall reproduce; what, how much and when the cat shall eat; when, where and how long the pet will sleep; what, if any, recreation it is allowed and when and where it will be allowed to urinate and defecate. Worse still, the human lays down these rules but is abysmally bad in making them clear to the feline, because humans simply don't think like cats.

Of course, cats will try to fit into your world. They are adaptable creatures and have managed to live with us for thousands of years in reasonable harmony.

But this adaptability doesn't alter your cat's basic reactions. Your cat won't change its nature to suit you. Cats don't *do* obedience – least of all for humans.

So, if the relationship isn't working out, it's you (not your cat) who will have to change. And to know what to do, you must learn cat rules. If possible, you must learn to think like a cat and understand the world through your cat's eyes. And the biggest difference between humans and cats is how they think of home. A house that is a happy home to its human occupant may not be a happy home to a cat.

Your home and your cat's home

For most of us humans, home has clear, fixed boundaries, and we mark these boundaries with solid walls. If we live in a flat, indoors is home and humans don't enter unless we let them. We control the space completely. If we live in a house with a garden, then there are the house walls and slightly different boundaries marked either by lower walls or by fences or hedges or wire netting. In open-plan estates, only a small line of shrubs mark the boundaries.

Yet we know they are there, even if we can step across them. The garden is our space. We control the garden boundaries, and other humans don't (or shouldn't) go into it unless we ask them in. We keep out of theirs.

But your cat doesn't recognize these boundaries at all. For a cat, there is a core home territory and a home range for hunting. A cat that spends some time out of doors usually recognizes indoors as more or less its core home territory. But it still doesn't really recognize the fact that physical boundaries, like walls or doors, mark territories.

These are obviously obstacles for cats, but they do not necessarily mean boundaries to them. This may be why cats make their humans into door-keepers, asking to be let out, only to insist on being let in again, a number of times. They don't recognize the meaning of doors, but see them merely as inconvenient obstacles. Going in and out reassures them that the outside hunting range is still open to them.

The most obvious example of the difference between you and your cat are the walls or hedges of your garden. You stay inside the walls and hedges, even though you could climb over them into your next-door neighbour's garden space. Your cat often pays no attention to them and may well, unless chased or frightened out, treat your neighbour's garden as part of its hunting range.

Your cat also has a different attitude to roads. You see a road as a pathway and also as a barrier. Pausing at the side of a road, you take care in crossing it. Your cat probably doesn't see the road as a pathway at all and it has only a vague sense of it as a barrier. Passing cars will make it pause before crossing while they are passing, but it has no sense of the potential danger from a car far off. If your cat lives near a main road, it will not hesitate to cross it to get to an attractive hunting ground at the other side. It simply doesn't recognize traffic danger. At night, when its eyes are dazzled by headlights, this will probably cost it its life.

Your cat has a smell map of its hunting range. Its territory is defined by scent markings left by itself: chin- or cheek-rubbing places, urine-spraying places or places where it leaves a faeces message. We know that cats don't rub where they spray, or spray where they rub, on the same place, but we still don't know exactly what is going on in a cat's mind when it marks its territory.

Your cat may avoid the places where a frightening local cat sprays, recognizing these spray marks as feline notices like 'Watch out – Kilroy is here' graffiti. Or it may spray over the existing mark, perhaps with the aim of blotting out the other cat's scent with its own.

'Muffy says if you're not busy later, come over to
our territory for supper.'

At other spray sites it will recognize messages left by more than one cat, marking areas where several cats share territory. It may add its own mark to the existing ones, not to blot them out, but to put an additional message there. These multiple spray-mark sites may be like a bulletin boards on the feline equivalent of a communal village green, where several cats can legitimately enjoy the area in common, though perhaps at different times. There may even be spray messages (perhaps from cats in season) which invite other cats to come up and see them sometime! Because we can't smell well, we can't be sure of their meanings.

Finally, your cat will also recognize visually and by scent scratch marks within its territory. The scent will have been left by the sweat glands of the scratching cat's paw pads. Your cat may add its own scratch to the site. The scratches may mean 'Kilroy was here' or simply 'Look at me: I scratch higher!'

Feeling home is safe – by smell

When a cat rubs, or sprays, or scratches, it feels better. The smell is usually reassuring – like the smell of home. Rubbing usually takes place where the cat feels happy and secure. Spraying is the way a cat tries to reassure itself by marking its territory, but if its anxiety does not diminish, it may spray over and over again.

A happy cat needs a safe home territory. It can usually live happily enough with a hunting range that overlaps with other cats; after all, pet cats don't need to hunt for food. But its core territory, where it sleeps, must be safe from intruding strangers, whether these are humans or animals.

This core territory has to smell right; it must smell of the cat itself. So your cat will go round its home making scent marks which are invisible to us humans: rubbing its chin and its cheek on various items in the house. A house is not a home until it smells of home. Only then can your cat feel relaxed.

Each time it rubs against a chair or a table leg, it leaves its own scent and picks up the scent of the household item. The home scent is a mixture of smells: your cat itself, the household furniture and the other living beings in the house. Where your cat leaves these invisible rubbing messages, it will not need to do any other scent marking – so it will not need to spray or leave a faeces message where it has rubbed.

Your cat will usually not need to scent mark its home by spraying (this only happens if it starts feeling insecure). But it will need to mark its home territory by scratching as well as rubbing. Your cat stands on its back legs at full height and rakes its legs down a vertical surface or does a horizontal scratch across a carpet. Scratching conditions its claws, but it also conveys a message, visual and scented, to other cats.

This scratching often occurs in front of a familiar cat companion or a familiar human – a 'Look at me' message. Certainly cats that scratch in front of humans often do so in order to get human attention – even if the attention is of the 'Stop doing that!' variety. Your cat probably knows that if it starts scratching the furniture, you will immediately look at it and say something rude. As an attention-seeking device, scratching works well!

Finally, your cat has to mix its scent with other family members. Remember, cat rules identify family mainly by scent, not sight. And anybody who doesn't smell like family is not welcome in its home territory. So your cat rubs up against you in a friendly way, partly to get your attention and partly to mix its scent. And when you pet it, you are following proper cat behaviour rules. By stroking your cat, you are leaving your scent on the cat. Your hand now smells of the cat and the cat now smells of your hand. From the cat's point of view, petting means that you are doing a friendly family-scent rub. You are, without realizing it, behaving like a cat should, and by doing so, you are strengthening the bond between you.

Cats will also rub against household dogs. If your cat met a family dog when it was a kitten, it will have no difficulty adapting to a dog in the household. Likewise, a dog that has met cats when it was a puppy will be relaxed around cats in the home. Both seem able to communicate, learning enough of each other's body language to get along.

Difficulties between dogs and cats will only arise when a cat which has never known dogs is forced to live with one. The worst-possible scenario for your cat will occur if it has to live with a dog which has been taught to chase cats in the past. A sensible cat, faced with ever-present danger in its core territory, will usually leave home.

If you take up with a new partner who comes with dogs to live in your home, you may welcome the dog, but your cat may not. You may have to think about re-homing your existing cat. Or, of course, you could re-home the partner!

Sharing with other cats

Not all cats enjoy living with other cats. Cats are not pack animals, like dogs. A kitten which never met any other cats except for its mother and siblings may not be keen in later life to live in a feline family with other cats. If your cat has spent its first adult months as a solitary pet in a household, it will find adapting to other cats very difficult indeed. Even if your cat was brought up as a kitten to get along with other cats, it may have difficulty when a new cat is introduced into your home. It is unlikely to greet the newcomer with anything other than hostility.

Any new cat smells wrong: like a foe, not a friend. The new arrival hasn't yet acquired the home smell of your house, and so your cat will automatically treat it as an intruder. Until it acquires the right home smell mixture, it will never be accepted by your existing cat. This can take several weeks. Indeed, if your existing cat has a solitary nature, it may never truly like its new companion. It will share its home territory with the newcomer, but their relationship will be one of armed neutrality, not friendship.

'Get lost!
I own this house!'

'You do? What
about Mr and
Mrs Dobson?'

'I own them, too!'

Conflict or harmony: scent rules

Scent can also sometimes lead to fights between cats that have hitherto been friends. A sudden antagonism may occur if one of your cats has returned home from time spent in another household, or has returned from the vet's surgery. It comes home smelling of the vet: a smell that is extremely upsetting. It smells *wrong* – badly wrong. As a result, its companion cat attacks it as if it were a strange intruder.

Although, as a human, you will never fully understand the importance of smell messages, you can now get help from the vet. Vets sell a product called Feliway, which is an artificial scent made to smell like the rubbing scent of a cat. Most humans can't detect the smell, but cats can – and it makes most cats feel more relaxed. It comes either in spray form or as a diffuser that is plugged into the mains.

So if you want to help your cat get used to a new feline companion, you can plug a Feliway diffuser into the room where both cats spend most of their time. The relaxing scent will last about a month and will reduce the tension between them. Or you can use the Feliway spray daily around the household cat pathways at feline chin height. There is also a similar product called Felifriend®, which is used by vets and cat workers to make their hand smell friendly to cats. If you spray this on your own hands and then stroke both cats, this, too, may help promote harmony between them. You can also add to the family scent mix by swapping the cats' bedding so that the two cats begin to smell of each other.

There is a cheaper alternative to Feliway, which is useful for cats that do not respond to it. Its only disadvantage is that it requires you to have the kind of cat that enjoys having its cheek and chin rubbed. Using a small piece of clean cloth (like a hanky), rub your cat's cheek and chin. Then using the same cloth, do the same to the new cat, transferring your existing cat's scent to the newcomer. Then transfer the new cat's scent back to your existing cat.

Do this twice daily for at least two weeks. This will only work if both cats are relaxed about the procedure. If rubbing cheek and chin with a hanky upsets either cat, it will only make things worse between them. If so, try the same trick with fingers only.

Finally, in order to maximize harmony between cats, it is important to have more than enough beds, food bowls and litter trays. There should be one litter tray for each cat and one over – just in case. This is particularly important if your cat is being harassed by one of its feline companions, which may be ambushing it on its way to or from the litter tray.

Cats also need hideaways if there are several cats in the house. Ideally, a house with many cats should include resting places high up on shelves, window-sills or even the top of cupboards.

All these measures will fail if you have too many cats. They aren't primarily social animals, and the more cats kept in a household, the more incidents of intimidation or fighting you're likely to have. Here are the signs to watch out for that show when a cat has become a victim of bullying in its own home.

•The victim needs veterinary treatment for bitten ears, broken skin, or abscesses after bites.

• The victim is afraid to enter the house and spends most of its time out of doors.

• The victim spends most of its time in hiding.

• The victim stops grooming itself.

• The victim is too frightened to eat when the others are in the feeding area.

• The victim is too fearful to use the litter tray and may soil the house.

• The victim is no longer willing to approach you, for fear of being attacked by the others.

• You see conflict signs: blood or tufts of fur.

• The aggressor patrols an area of the house so that the victim only has a small bit of living space.

If any one of these signs is evident, seek help from a pet behaviour counsellor. More than one sign, or if expert help fails, and you must consider re-homing the victim cat. No cat should live a life of constant fear. Put its happiness before your own.

'You smell horrible!'

'Well, you're not exactly
Chanel No. 5…'

Litter-tray etiquette

A feeling of safety when using the litter tray is essential to a cat's feeling of happiness within its core home territory. Cats are usually taught their toilet arrangements by their mother. Most pet cats will be familiar with a particular kind of litter. Kittens that have started life out of doors, however, may be used to soil or sand – as may stray adult cats that have lived rough for a long time.

The actual type of litter is important, because the feel of it under its paws will trigger your cat's desire to use it. It's just like wanting to go the bathroom but not 'being there'; when we are safely on the seat does the feel of the seat allows us to put the urge into action.

A cat that has been used to soil under its paws will not be happy with the different feel of commercial litter. So, when getting a new cat or a new kitten, it is important to start with the kind of litter they are used to. A stray cat may need soil or builder's sand in the litter tray. If you ever want to change to a different type of litter, do this slowly – handful by handful – over several weeks. On the whole cats prefer expensive, fine-grained litter to coarse ones. Heavy wood litters or light litters made by recycled newspapers are unpopular with some cats.

It is essential that your cat is happy with its litter tray. An unhappy cat will go outside the tray. so it is in your interests to make sure your cat is happy.

Not only does your cat need familiar litter, it also needs a safe place for the litter tray. Cats do not like to use a litter tray in the feeding or sleeping area, so the litter tray must be some distance from the food bowl and the bed. It should also be in a relatively secluded area – not in a place where humans or other pets are often walking by. Cats feel vulnerable when they are using the tray. A covered tray can help. Before buying a covered one, experiment with a cardboard box with a hole cut in it – just in case yours is the rare animal that prefers an open tray.

Your cat will also prefer clean litter. It does not like having to dig through soiled litter, so clean the tray at least twice a day. If you can't do this, set up a second tray for each cat so that no tray gets too dirty. Be generous, not stingy, with litter; after all, your cat may like a good dig. Do not use a deodorant litter or a sprayed-on deodorant. This makes the litter tray smell wrong to some cats. Your cat likes a clean tray that nonetheless smells ever so slightly like a latrine.

If a sensitive cat starts to refuse to use a litter tray used by its companion cat, then add extra litter trays. Or if it refuses to use the same tray for both urination and defecation, install two trays: one for one, the other for the other.

Finally, if a cat has a bad experience while it is on the litter tray, it may take against the tray itself. Bad experiences include abdominal pain while using the tray, cystitis pain, being ambushed while on the tray by another cat, fear because of a sudden loud noise, fear because of some other unexpected occurrence. The cat blames the tray for this. Buy a new tray.

Your cat may also stop using its tray if you change the position of the tray itself. If this happens, put the tray back to its original position, let the cat use it there for about a week, and then move it about six inches a day towards the new position.

Occasionally your cat's ability to use the litter tray may seem to break down altogether. Your cat soils the house all over the place and does not respond to better litter-tray arrangements. Always check with the vet in case the animal is ill. If not, it helps to call in a pet behaviour counsellor, via your vet, who can give expert advice after seeing you, the cat and the house!

If all this seems like too much trouble, then remember, it is in your own best interests to keep your cat happy and therefore house-trained. Anything, but anything, is better than a house smelling of cat pee!

'Put the snake away now, darling.
You're stressing Timmy.'

chapter six
HELP! STRESS, FEARS, EATING
DISORDERS AND AGGRESSION

Considering how different our two species are, the relationship between humans and cats works extraordinarily well – most of the time. Humans give food and shelter, and cats take food and shelter. All they are required to do is to repay their humans with affection and the grace of their presence.

Three or four generations ago, cats were kept primarily as rodent operatives, fed just a little, but expected to earn their keep hunting mice. Nowadays, cats are often a human's best friends. They fit into modern life rather better than dogs. Cats don't bark or make a noise. Cats don't need daily exercise. Cats are clean in their toilet habits.

When your relationship with your cat does run into trouble, it is usually in four areas: toilet arrangements, scratching, eating or aggression. The first difficulty is the most severe one.

Marking territory – a cry for help

If cats suddenly start going to the toilet outside its litter tray, a medical problem may be the cause. Sometimes, as discussed earlier, cats are not happy with the litter-tray arrangements. But often cats go outside the litter tray because they have started marking their territory.

You can tell the difference by the location of the marks. A cat which is going outside its litter tray because it is unhappy about the toilet arrangements will usually go either near the tray (or near its old position) or in a secluded place like behind furniture. A cat that is territory marking will urinate in a more obvious position and the urine mark will usually be on a vertical rather than a horizontal object. If you see them doing it, they are usually spraying urine from a standing, not a squatting, position.

If your cat feels that its core territory is no longer safe, it will respond by setting up stronger territory marks within the house. It will start leaving 'I was here' scent notices to deter other cats, dogs, wildlife or human intruders. These notices are usually urine marks made by spraying, but they may also be faeces left uncovered in a prominent place.

These scent marks are a sign of your cat's anxiety. Sadly, we humans rarely recognize these 'I was here' messages for what they are. We often react with anger and alarm rather than love and comfort. Some owners interpret them as insults. Other owners get so upset that they punish the cat. Naturally, the cat is now even more frightened. Its home feels positively dangerous when it is shared with a punishing human. The cat responds in the only way it knows: by putting up more and stronger scent messages.

We can learn to interpret some of the messages by taking a careful look at where the messages occur. If the cat is leaving spray marks or faeces under or near the window, the likelihood is that something in the garden outside is frightening. Maybe through the window it can see a fox or a local cat bully. Marks at the inside of a door may have been left because your cat can smell dogs or other cats which have passed by or even urine-marked on the other side.

Another common reason for marking is when an intruding cat uses the cat flap – often a hungry stray coming in to steal your cat's dinner. Naturally your cat is upset by this intrusion into its own core territory. It may spray near the cat flap or, if it is horribly upset, it may go upstairs and do it on your bed. Humans often think this is an insult, but just the reverse is true. The cat, anxious and insecure, is going to the place that smells of its loved one. It mixes its scent with your odour. Cats that go on the bed are telling you that they love you and they need your help.

Other intruders that upset cats include builders, friends or people you have invited to a party. Even cat-sitters or neighbours coming in to feed the cat while you are away can be upsetting. Normally, your cat may be friendly to the woman next door. It may greet her happily when she is in her garden. But if she comes into the house when you are away, even to leave regular food, a sensitive cat may feel she is intruding into its private space. Other upsetting occurrences for sensitive cats include new furniture, a new baby or even sudden changes in routine (for instance, if their owner starts working night shifts).

If you have more than one cat, then your first task must be to discover which of your cats is doing the marking. Do not assume you know, unless you have seen the behaviour. There is a fluorescent dye which can be fed in a cat's food that will show up in the spray marks, thus making it clear which cat is spraying. Get this from your vet.

Next, clean up the territory marks. Wash or dry-clean materials; never use disinfectants or any scented household liquids on floors or carpets. Instead, scrub with biological washing powder or liquid, or with products sold by a vet. Then rinse the area with plain water – this is important. Finally, let the area dry or dry it with a hair dryer, and then scrub over again with surgical spirit. This also is important. Unless the area is thoroughly cleaned, your cat will re-mark it!

There should then be a delay of up to twenty-four to forty-eight hours, after which you should either use Feliway on the marking sites or the scent

'Denise! The cat's been
spraying the furniture again!'

off your cat's cheek and chin as described in chapter five. If you cannot keep your cat away from the spray areas for as long as twenty-four hours, put some cling film over the cleaned area and use Feliway immediately on the cling film.

Cats do not rub where they have sprayed and, conversely, they do not spray where they have rubbed. So if the mark site smells of chin or Feliway, they will not urine-spray it. Use the Feliway spray lavishly twice daily for at least a month. If you are stingy with it, it may not work. Also, install a Feliway diffuser in the relevant room.

In addition to Feliway or your cat's own scent (but not as a substitute for them), other helpful measures include putting cat beds and cat feeding bowls at the spray sites. Stick bits of dry food onto cardboard squares and fix these against the wall. Cats don't like to spray where they dine or sleep. Consider using double-sided sticky tape on the areas where the cat would stand to spray; cats dislike sticky surfaces.

Stress points for your cat

In the United States, drugs are sometimes used to treat spraying cats. This is rare in Britain. Even with drugs, it is essential to find out what has stressed the cat, and then correct the situation. Work your way through this list of feline stress points. If you are still not sure what is going on, get expert help from a pet behaviour counsellor.

Fear of other outside cats, dogs or wildlife
Stop leaving food down indoors or close cat flap. Wash down the outside of doors daily to clean up any smells left by neighbouring cats. If necessary, place wire netting or Prickler® wall strips near the front door and put prominent plant pots about three yards away in the hope that the local cats or dogs will mark these rather than the door area. Use Feliway inside the house, especially near doors and windows.

Sight of cats/wildlife/dogs
Block off the sight of the potential threat temporarily by covering the window with cardboard. If this is effective, make it permanent by using the spray sold

in DIY shops for frosting bathroom windows. Stop strange cats staring in from window-boxes, -sills or nearby walls by covering these with wire netting or Prickler wall strips. Use Feliway indoors near the window area.

Fear of indoor cats
There may simply be too many cats, leading to fights, ambushes or bullying. Other causes of stress include new cats and cats in season or kittening. Make sure there are more than enough litter trays, beds, food bowls and hideaways. For a long-term solution, get advice from a behaviour counsellor.

New objects
Treat new objects with Feliway or mark them with the cat's own scent from cheek or chin before the cat has contact with them. Continue the Feliway daily for a week to a fortnight.

Whatever it is, I don't want it.

Shopping bags

Cats sometimes spray on these because the shopping bag has been put down on the doorstep while the shopper opens the front door. If neighbouring cats spray on the doorstep, then the shopping bag smells of their urine. Leave the bags in the car until you have opened the door.

Builders and decorators

Keep the cat away from the altered rooms until paint smells, etc., have died down. Or put your cat in a cattery during building works. Use Feliway or the cat's own scent in the newly decorated room or in the new house before your cat enters.

Visitors

Occasionally cats will spray after visitors. Consider a cattery at Christmas, party times or during visits. Do not allow visitors to bring dogs.

Cat feeders or home sitters

Consider using a cattery instead of sitters.

Attention-seeking spraying
You need expert help for this. This method of getting attention really, really works and it helps to have an expert mind working out how to stop it.

New cat flap
Get rid of this or shut it down.

Electrical items or warm radiators
When they heat up, they may emit odours which prompt spraying. Move the item, if possible. Try Feliway if you can use it safely, or install a Feliway Diffuser plug in the room.

Companion cat illness
A medical problem in the cat's companion cat may produce spraying. Check the state of the companion cat's health as well as that of the spraying cat.

Scratching the furniture to shreds

The other less difficult, though irritating, territory mark is the scratch. Scratching is natural for all cats and takes place even if the cat feels perfectly at ease. The trick is to give the cat several large, steady scratching posts in the house, and discourage scratching elsewhere. The best scratching posts are covered with sisal, rather than carpet. One may not be enough; scratching posts should be installed in any room where the cat scratches.

In the United States, it is considered acceptable to de-claw a cat that scratches furniture. This operation is not performed in Britain and it would leave outdoor cats vulnerable to injury, since it severely reduces their ability to climb fences and trees. Cats also scratch when they are stressed, so consult the stress-points mentioned earlier.

Double-sided sticky tape is the best way to stop furniture scratching. The cat stops scratching because it hates getting its paws sticky and, after a week or two, the tape can be removed – though new tape may be needed when the cat realizes the furniture is free from sticky tape. Taping your furniture looks bad, but not as bad as having it hang in shreds.

Horizontal surfaces such as carpets can be covered with see-through plastic from a DIY shop, double-sided tape, cooking foil, or wire netting. A scratching post should be installed nearby as a substitute place to scratch. Cats that scratch wallpaper can be discouraged by the daily use of Feliway or the scent of their own chin put on the scratch site.

OK - this is war!

Some cats scratch outside doors in order to let their owners know they want to be let in. One way to stop this behaviour is never, ever, to let the cat in when it has scratched. It should only be let in when it has not scratched. This requires a high level of human consistency to match the persistence of the scratching cat. Placing double-sided tape on the area where the cat scratches; just outside the door might be easier and just as effective.

Shouting at a scratching cat is not a good idea. Cats often scratch in front of other cats, possibly in a competitive way of saying, 'Look at me: I can scratch higher than you!' Your cat may also scratch in front of you, glancing sideways to see if this gets your attention. Shouting 'Stop that!' is attention, and bad attention is better than no attention. So if you think your cat is using scratching as an attention-seeking device, walk immediately out of the room. Do not use a water pistol. A cat that is squirted in its home territory may begin to feel unsafe and start spraying – and nothing is worse than a spraying cat!

Weird appetites and eating disorders

Most cats regulate their food intake better than humans do, but the feline world does include overeaters, often encouraged by their doting owners. Overeating cats take less exercise and have more interest in food than ordinary cats. If your cat gets too fat, put it on a diet available from your vet, limit its intake, and do not weaken. Most fat cats have a human enabler. Offer games instead of food.

However, there are cats which have a serious eating disorder. These are the cats that eat strange substances such as cardboard or wool, cats that chew and rip but don't swallow, and cats that just lick these odd materials. If your cat starts doing this, or even starts eating its litter, take it to the vet, because a bizarre appetite may be a sign of physical illness.

If your cat is in good health, however, eating strange things like wool or cotton is more likely to be a disorder of the feline natural hunting instinct. Siamese or related breeds are particularly prone to this behaviour, as are indoor cats that have no chance to hunt prey.

Remember the hunting sequence of eye, stalk, pounce, bite, tear off skin or feathers, and eat? The wool or cardboard eaters are cats that have become compulsive about one part of the predatory sequence: tearing off skin or feathers. Some just tear and pluck and do not swallow. Others tear and pluck and then eat. Since ordinary cat food gives no opportunity for tearing and ripping, the cat looks for something else to satisfy this urge. It will tear, rip, chew and sometimes eat wool, cotton, paper, cardboard, wicker baskets, electric cables. Those cats that simply rip, tear, chew and then spit out do little harm to themselves, but those that actually swallow these inappropriate substances risk an internal blockage, which will require an operation.

The treatment for this behaviour is to give your cat the chance to tear and shred by feeding it either dead, whole feathered turkey chicks, dead day-old chicks, dead whole rats, or dead furry mice (not the baby pinkies) sold frozen by pet shops for reptiles. Or, if all else fails, buy hens with their feathers still on from a local farm shop. Wash your hands before and after feeding this diet, because, as reptile keepers know, there is a slight chance of salmonella.

These should be the cat's main diet, eaten in a room such as a bathroom where blood won't get on the carpet. If you want to add a little dry food on top of this (only a minority part of the diet), do so in a foraging toy, where the cat has to work to get the dried food out. Although the whole idea is disgusting to humans, this may be the only way to cure your cat of a dangerous disorder.

Because this weird behaviour is part of the hunting sequence gone wrong, it may also help to give your cat the chance to hunt, either by allowing it out of doors or by giving it a lot of predatory games where it can stalk and pounce on toys.

Owners whose cats merely tear and chew, rather than swallow weird substances, sometimes find the disorder amusing. By laughing at the cat and giving it attention, they encourage its behaviour. The danger is that, if your cat is merely tearing and

'You've got to stop eating junk!'

chewing, it may be encouraged to go further and start swallowing. So be careful to withdraw attention from a cat that is tearing and chewing. This takes nerve if your cat is chewing electric cables. But, shouting 'No!', rushing over to it or picking it up will only encourage it, since all these moves are human attention. Instead, leave the room.

As well as trying to cure this chewing by withdrawing attention, you can cover wires with plastic tubes from the DIY shop. Try spraying cables with an anti-animal product sold for gardeners. Try giving your cat dog chews or, if necessary, some dead chicks in the diet as described in the previous pages.

It is worth taking action at the first sign of this disorder for fear that tearing and chewing will lead to weird eating.

Biting the hand that feeds him

In normal circumstances cats rarely attack humans. If they dislike a person, they are far more likely simply to make themselves scarce. If a previously calm cat suddenly turns aggressive, it is essential that you take it to the vet. A sick cat or a cat in pain may bite when handled. There may be a hidden abscess. Pregnant cats or cats with litters are also sometimes aggressive in defence of their litters.

A kitten that is brought up in the wild will never become wholly domesticated. These unsocialized strays may learn to live in the house, but they may continue to bite from fear when handled.

The petting and biting syndrome

This is the most common occasion when otherwise friendly cats bite. Petting is enjoyable to humans, but less enjoyable to cats. It relaxes us, but it can stress some cats. If your cat bites when being petted, it is in conflict – it wants attention but fears it, too. Your cat may want contact and love, but after a time it gets frightened. At this point, it bites or scratches.

This may be the result of a dysfunctional kitten-hood, and probably this kind of cat's desire for space should be respected. Some stray cats, however, were once domestic kittens in a home but then lived rough as strays and suffered at the hands of man. These cats, after months in a safe new home, may accept petting more easily in time. But never hurry them.

Some cats have sensitive areas (usually tummy and hindquarters) which produce aggression when touched. Avoid these. Long-haired cats may have been roughly groomed in the past and be more likely to bite or scratch if they feel threatened. In chapter four, I give instructions on how to get them used to grooming again.

If you want to try to change this petting-and-biting behaviour, use special treats as a reward for calmness. Show your cat the treat first, then give it a little bit of petting: just calm stroking nowhere near its tummy. Your cat will be focusing on the food.

Give the treat after only a very short period of petting. If your cat swipes a claw at you, then it doesn't get the treat it has been shown. This way, calmness under petting, rather than aggression, is rewarded. Slowly increase the petting time, always making sure your cat sees the treat on offer before you start.

In general only pet your cat when it can get away: i.e. with no enclosed arms and probably not on a lap. Do not pick it up. Try stroking only the head and down the back. Always let the cat remove itself when it has had enough. You could also make your hand smell friendly by using Felifriend spray from the vet.

Develop your relationship in other ways. Non-cuddly cats enjoy play; have regular play sessions with string, fishing rods, etc. Also, use food treats to train a cat to do simple tricks of a kind it enjoys. Greedy cats will actually solicit training sessions!

Predatory aggression
If cats don't have enough to do (and indoor cats usually don't), attacking humans is a substitute for hunting mice. Pouncing and attacking is instinctive behaviour for cats and they really enjoy it. Give your cat more to do according to the instructions in chapter four.

'I could get quite used to these liqueur
chocolates she trains me with.'

If your cat already goes outside but just enjoys pouncing on you, use sound as a discourager. Ring a small bell each time you start vacuuming (assuming your cat loathes the vacuum cleaner; most do). Then use the bell when you see the cat about to pounce on you. Timing is important. The aim is to deter your cat from pouncing, without it becoming frightened of you. Sound can be used in such a way that the cat may not be entirely sure that you are making it.

If your cat attacks neighbours, just give them a water pistol and ask them to use it. It doesn't matter if your cat associates them with the water pistol.

Frustration aggression
Hand-reared kittens are sometimes unable to tolerate frustration because they were not weaned in the proper way. Kittens learn to tolerate frustration when their mother starts pushing them away from the teats. As the bottle is never withheld by a human, they are never frustrated.

Thus, hand-reared cats have no emotional control because they were not put through this process. They have no coping strategy for frustration so just lash out. They control their owners by this. Their aggression is effective as the owner naturally backs away.

Turn the relationship around by clicker training or reward training; you start controlling the cat, instead of the cat controlling you. Attach a soft object (like an old stuffed sock) to a stick, so that you can use this to push the cat off a chair and avoid getting hurt.

Aggressive play

Sometimes people encourage kittens to do rough games then dislike it when the grown-up cat wields a stronger claw or more painful bite. But by then the cat has rough games in its repertoire. The rule is that games stop immediately if your cat hurts you.

Attention-seeking biting

Some cats nip their owner's legs when they want something. The answer is to withdraw attention. Don't shout, don't wince, don't cry. (You may have to wear boots in the house in order to avoid any response to the pain.) Just walk out of the room immediately and stay out for three or four minutes. Attention-seeking biting will stop if it no longer gets attention.

Transferred aggression

Occasionally an otherwise docile cat will attack its owners because it is aroused by something else. For instance, if it is watching another cat through the window, it may turn on them. It cannot help itself; its excited aggression has to be expressed – on the nearest person. If you interrupt a cat fight, you will get bitten.

'The cat's in a foul mood, dear.
Can you get him off me?'

chapter seven
OLD AGE: PAMPERING YOUR ELDERLY CAT

There is something immensely touching about the elderly cat; stiff from arthritis, and probably with several teeth missing, it has a tendency to nap often and everywhere. Yet it still retains the remnants of grace and the serenity of a purr.

Old cats show a wonderful ability to manage their humans. Many devoted owners find themselves becoming obedient servants to their elderly felines – moving over in the bed to offer more room under the duvet, holding the cat's tail or stroking it while it eats, giving up the warmest chairs near the radiators, and generally responding to elderly vocal demands for instant attention.

There is no need for embarrassment about this. Your cat probably feels that this is its right as a member (in its eyes) of a superior species. There is nothing like an elderly feline to put a human in its place: which is, of course, well below that of the cat!

Old cats are still cats, even if in their golden years they no longer haunt the hedges and fields to hunt mice or go on long hunting expeditions in search of rabbits. If it enjoyed hunting in its prime, however, an old cat will still hunt butterflies in the garden or perhaps bluebottles on the window-pane. The instinct to hunt is still alive even if the prey is much smaller.

Old age does not alter personality much, either. A naturally aloof cat may become somewhat less independent but it will not turn into a cuddly, soft toy of a feline. A lap cat may become more clinging. There is a sweetness that can appear in old age, in which a cat draws closer to its human.

'As you get older, your memory goes…'

'So you keep telling me.'

Giving your cat a long life

Cats, like humans, live longer nowadays. If they avoid dangerous infections and fatal disorders, and do not get run over by cars, they can often reach the age of fifteen. A few with super-survivor genes get past the age of twenty and may even pass their third decade. A cat aged twenty is more or less the equivalent of a ninety-year-old human.

If you want your cat to survive into old age, then vaccination is essential if it is allowed out of the house. It is now possible to vaccinate against feline leukaemia as well as cat flu and feline panleucopaenia, a kind of viral gastro-enteritis.

There is also a vaccine against chlamydia that is useful if your cat lives in an area full of disease-ridden strays. If you are a cat rescuer likely to have stray cats passing through your house on the way to a rescue shelter, your own cats should be protected by chlamydia vaccinations.

How to protect against illness

The other essential way of keeping a cat healthy into its old age is prompt treatment by a vet for any wounds or diseases. In the past, both cats and dogs were often put down because their owners could not, or did not want to, pay out large sums for veterinary treatment.

Pet insurance has benefited many cats and dogs, making veterinary treatment affordable even for people on a relatively small income. Choose an insurer that will continue to insure your cat after the age of eight. No insurer will take on an already elderly cat, and some of the cheaper insurers refuse to insure animals after the age of eight. In this, as in other areas of life, you get what you pay for.

On the more positive side, health care for cats has improved immeasurably in the last decade, and it is now possible to measure cat blood pressure and detect many diseases in their early stages. Most good veterinary clinics offer not just regular vaccinations, but regular health checks for elderly cats. Blood tests can detect the early stages of kidney disease, liver disease and thyroid disease. This preventive treatment is not covered by insurance, but any subsequent veterinary treatment needed as a result of these tests will be.

Finally, do not hesitate to seek a second opinion for all serious or chronic health problems. Just as general-practitioner doctors refer patients to specialist consultants, so ordinary vets can refer their animal patients to specialist vets.

This is a much more effective way of getting additional help for a cat with a specific health problem than simply changing vets. The veterinary department of the local university or a nearby specialist veterinary hospital will often be able to offer more up-to-date diagnostic assessment and treatment. Pet insurance will usually pay for this.

Prompt treatment of disease is essential for emotional and mental well being in old age – both for humans and for cats. Sick cats or cats in pain suffer emotionally as well as physically, which in turn affects their mental capacity to cope.

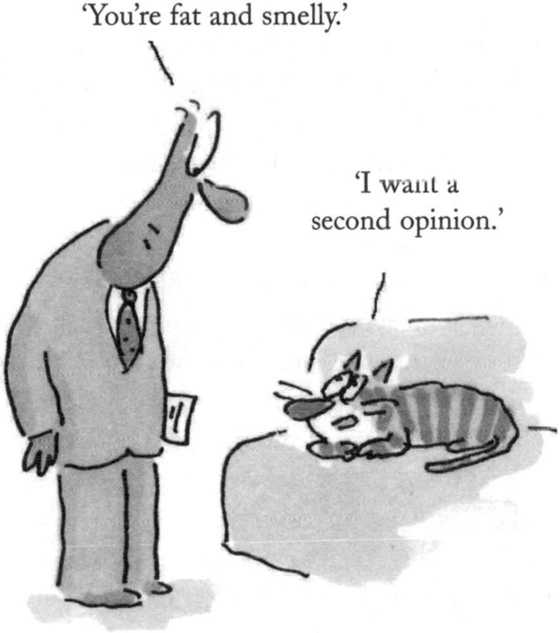
'You're fat and smelly.'
'I want a second opinion.'

Feline body maintenance

Proper control of parasites also benefits cats. Regular worming against tapeworm is important for cats that catch mice. Regular flea treatment is also needed, since tapeworms are spread via fleas.

Most people don't realize that treating the animal itself for parasites is not enough. It is essential to treat the house at regular intervals, too. Otherwise, a reservoir of flea eggs and larvae remain unharmed and will grow up into adult fleas. Most owners nevertheless still don't treat the house, confining themselves to treating the pet alone. Fortunately, there are now very effective anti-flea preparations, many of them with growth inhibitors that attack the flea's ability to reproduce.

Tooth care is the other area where most of us owners fall short. Middle-aged cats, like middle-aged people, often develop dental problems. Their teeth get coated with calculus, a hard deposit that eventually inflames the gums. Each time your cat is vaccinated, your vet should check the condition of its teeth.

In theory, it is possible to learn how to brush your cat's teeth and now that there are meat-flavoured toothpastes, your cat will tolerate brushing if it is introduced to it as a kitten. Unfortunately, this practice does require considerable human determination since the brush has to be stuffed right into the cat's mouth.

Failing regular brushing, consider a dental-cleaning food or regular dental chews. Your cat's teeth can also be cleaned under an anaesthetic.

If your cat seems keen to eat, but draws back when it starts eating, the cause might be tooth pain. Cats with a history of cat flu sometimes develop chronic gingivitis (gum inflammation). This can make eating, which should be a pleasure, a real pain. Use of steroids or even complete extraction of all teeth may be the treatments of last resort.

There are specialist dental vets, either with clinics of their own, or who visit veterinary clinics on a regular basis. Ask for your cat to be seen by one of these if it has continuing dental difficulties.

Feeding to prolong your cat's life

Special diets are now available for elderly cats or for cats with health problems or digestive troubles. Some of these are prescription diets, available only from vets, designed for cats with a continuing ailment such as kidney disease, or cystitis, allergy or food intolerance, bowel or digestive difficulties. These are all valuable contributions towards feline health. Alas, pet insurance will rarely cover the cost of a continuing special diet, but nonetheless, the correct diet will help your cat stay healthier and live longer.

There are also prescription diets for cats that need to lose weight. In general, most cats seem able to balance their diet so that they eat what they need without getting fat. Yet a small proportion of cats are fatties. Most veterinary clinics have weighing machines. Weigh your cat in its carrier on the scales, and then come back on a different occasion and weigh your cat carrier, subtracting this figure from the earlier one.

Fat cats are more likely to suffer from diabetes, and too much weight will worsen diseases such as arthritis and breathing difficulties. Just like fat humans, fat cats become less energetic, so they do less, and put on even more weight. Food may become of central importance in their lives, and they start living to eat. Doting owners contribute to their obesity by sharing their human meals (even curry!) with their furry fat friend. For us, eating is a social activity and we may therefore offer food as a proof of love – so the cat also starts treating food is a substitute for human attention.

This is called enabling. We owners with fat cats enable them to stay that way by letting – even encouraging – them to eat too much. The only kind action is to put the cat on a diet, always under veterinary supervision, and limit its food intake rigorously. As exercise will also help fatties slim down, we should learn to respond to cats with games in the place of food.

Never starve a fat cat. If a fat cat suddenly stops eating, its liver function may fail altogether. Weight should be lost gradually. Prescription diet foods, usually bulked out by extra fibre, weighed out in a daily portion, are the best way of slimming down a fatty.

A new slimming diet may need to be introduced gradually and mixed with the previous food to ensure that it's being eaten. If your cat regularly supplements its diet by entering other houses and raiding other cats' food, or turning over the local dustbins, it may need to be an indoor cat while it diets.

Special care for a special cat

Whatever its size, your cat has probably become more vocal in old age. Cats learn that humans respond to sound rather than body language so they use sound more often. Your cat may also use particular meows for particular demands – a language it has invented just for you. The more you respond, the more it will do this. Even previously silent cats may start to venture a few feline vocal remarks.

If your cat begins to wail and becomes restless, it should be checked for thyroid disease by a vet. Sometimes very old cats cry in the night, probably out of geriatric anxiety and a desire for a cuddle.

Elderly cats also sleep longer and more often. One conscientious feline researcher did a day's study-watch on an elderly cat, staying awake and noting all its movements for a full twenty-four hours. While the researcher struggled to stay awake, the cat slept in peaceful serenity for sixteen of those hours!

'Meouch!'

Coping with pain

Some elderly cats, by no means the majority, suffer from arthritis. *Never* give your cat a human painkiller, since cats react differently to drugs than humans. If you do try this, you may actually end up poisoning your cat. However a vet can prescribe appropriate drugs to reduce pain.

You can also provide ramps up to high places, and site beds and food bowls carefully. A heated pad or even a heated tunnel provides comfort for stiff and ageing limbs. If you can't get your cat its own heated bed, prepare to share, not just the outside, but also the inside of your own bed.

Elderly cats will also need help with grooming. They may no longer be able to reach difficult areas such as along the back. Long-haired cats should be groomed daily anyway. It is also necessary to keep an eye on an elderly cat's claws. Regular clipping may be necessary, so ask your vet to show you how.

Reducing stress

Many old cats adapt surprisingly well to a change of circumstances. The idea that an elderly cat will be unable to handle a change of house or routine or a new human in the household is unfounded. Elderly cats in good health seem to be able to handle the change surprisingly well, and to thrive in the new environment. There is no real reason, therefore, why older cats should be put down or euthanized when their owners die. Given the chance, they will settle into a new home – if one can be found.

Change they can handle, but not a huge amount of stress. Expecting an elderly cat to accept a dog in the household, if they have never lived with one, is cruel. Likewise, a new kitten with its playfulness may be too much for them. Your cat's early history will make a difference here. If it was brought up in a crowded cat household and has been used to the company of other cats in its present home, even in old age it may be able to adapt to a newcomer.

Stress for the elderly can be diminished by the lavish use of Feliway and the sensible use of a familiar cattery if the household is being disrupted by building works. Use the same cattery each visit and supply your own Feliway spray for the cattery owner to use.

The last gift you can give your cat

The last gift of love is euthanasia. Do not strive unnecessarily to keep alive a very old or very ill cat. All cats hate going to see a vet, and too much veterinary treatment can be as cruel as too little.

To human patients, medical treatment is painful but they know why it is being given. To cats, too much veterinary treatment can be torture. Veterinary treatment may buy extra time, but the extra time may not always have a good quality of life for the cat. It is important to put the cat's welfare before your own wishes.

These are the questions you need to ask to decide if your cat has a good quality of life.

•Is your cat still enjoying its food?

•Does your cat still play if you invite it to do so?

•Is it able to control its bowel or bladder?

•Can it get to its litter tray, to its food bowl and to its bed without too much difficulty?

•Can it still groom the easy-to-reach areas of its body?

•Is it suffering from frequent fits, vomiting or other chronic disorders?

•Is it in pain? Cats in pain sit hunched-up, avoid human contact, and may hiss or complain if touched.

•Does it require repeated veterinary interventions or stressful procedures such as injections, special feeding or pill-giving?

•What does your vet recommend?

Asking these questions – and giving honest answers – is the final gift you can give your cat.

'The cleaning lady knows someone whose
cat has just had a litter...'

'I can't complain, Felix. At least
they never bought a dog.'

appendix
DISABLED CATS

There was a time when disabled cats were almost always put down. But nowadays we realize that disabled cats, like disabled people, can lead happy lives. In most ways, they function just like healthy cats – only they need a bit more help from their humans.

Most disabled cats need to be kept indoors, or with access only to a high-fenced garden. They are more vulnerable to traffic, dogs and predators, even when they are in home territory.

Deaf cats

Deaf cats respond well to hand signs, so choose your own signs but be consistent; cats use body language in preference to sound language anyway. They also often respond to vibrations. Try clapping hands with your palms slightly cupped. This makes a vibration which the cat may 'hear' through its body. To recall a cat from the garden in the dark, use a torch to flash the signal.

Blind cats

Blind cats cope better than blind humans because they have superior hearing and superior scenting abilities. Whiskers will also become feelers for new territory. Remember to use voice and sound signals, not visual signs for these.

A special study of blind cats concluded that they had no difficulty making their needs known! Sometimes when disoriented they would just sit and howl until somebody picked them up. They still knew where the fridge (and food) was. Blind cats even played (toys with a little bell attached) and used the litter tray (probably scent helped here) as long as it was kept in the same place.

You can make life easier for your blind cat by keeping the furniture and the litter tray in the same place. Cats are incredibly good at mapping out areas and learn their own home area rapidly. Leave doors either shut or fully open; half-open and the cat can bump into them. Use fire-guards near all open fires.

Other disabilities

Wobbly cats with poor coordination, rickety gaits, sight problems, spasms, deformed front legs, or any other odd ways of walking can also lead enjoyable lives if looked after properly by kind humans. Litter trays must be wobble-free, since puss may need to lean against a side while using it.

Even cats with urinary incontinence – as a result, perhaps, of a car accident – can be helped to live out their lives if their humans are given proper advice and training. It is possible to learn how to express the urine by human hand. Get your vet to demonstrate.

Useful contacts

UK

For good information about feline diseases, UK boarding, rescue, and some feline behaviour problems, contact the Feline Advisory Bureau, Taeselbury, High St, Tisbury, Wilts SP3 6LD. Tel: 01747 871872.
Website www.fabcats.org

The Association of Pet Behaviour Counsellors,
PO Box 46, Worcester WR8 9YS.
Tel: 01386 751151. Web: www.apbc.org.uk
Vet's referral required. A counsellor will visit your home to assess the problem.

For cat and dog behaviour courses and books:
The Centre of Applied Pet Ethology,
PO Box 6, Fortrose, Ross-shire IV10 8WB.
Tel: 0800 783 0817. For courses: www.coape.co.uk.
For books: www.pet.f9.co.uk

For a kitten socialization pack, contact:
Headstart for Kittens, The Blue Cross,
Shilton Rd, Burford OX18 4PF. Tel: 01993 825500.
Web: www.bluecross. org.uk

Bereavement helpline: the SCAS Blue Cross line on tel: 0800 096 6606 will help you come to terms with losing your pet.

My own website, www.celiahaddon.co.uk, offers help with problems and a special section on disabled pets.

USA

Cornell Veterinary Education has useful brochures. Web: http://web.vet.cornell.edu/Public/FHC/brochure.html

Good Cats Wear Black. The US website of Annie Bruce, author of *Cat be Good*, and cat owner consultant. Annie campaigns against de-clawing.
Web: www.goodcatswearblack.com.

The Humane Society of the United States
www.hsus.org

Pet Place. A good general US website with useful facts about cats. Web: www.petplace.com

INDEX